What's that Sound?
Transportation Sounds

Kristi Nielsen

First of all thank you for purchasing "What's That Sound? "
It would really be appreiated if you would tell your friends and family about this book by posting to Facebook, Twitter or other Social Media.

Please post a review on Amazon. Your feedback and support will help the author greatly and make future books better. While you are on Amazon, check out other books by this author.

Your support is most appreciated. Thanks again.

This book is dedicated to my grandchildren and written and illustrated for all children to enjoy.
Support children's literacy. Reading books to children is important.

This work is fiction. Names, characters, places and incidents are products of the author's imagination.

All rights reserved. No part of this book may be reproduced, transmitted, or stored in an information retrieval system in any form or by any means, graphic, electronic, or mechanical, including photocopying, taping, and recording, without prior written permission from the author.

© Kristi Nielsen 2020

Electronic book: 978-1-989607-31-2 What's That Sound? Transportation Sounds

Paperback Book: 978-1-989607-27-5 What's That Sound? Transportation Sounds

WOOOOOOOOO
WOOOOOOOOH

HONK HONK

WOOOOOOOOO
WOOOOOOOOH

What's that sound?

It's a fire engine.

Whomp - whomp
whomp - whomp
whomp - whomp

What's that sound?

It's a helicopter.

Nee - Naw
   Nee - Naw
      Nee - Naw
         Nee - Naw

What's that sound?

It's an ambulance.

oo - oo - oo
oo - oo - oo
oo - oo - oo

What's that sound?

It's an airplane.

Brump brump brump brump brump

What's that sound?

It's a tractor.

Vroom – vroom
Vroom – vroom

What's that sound?

It's a car.

Beep - beep

- whirrfftt

- bonk - beep - beep

- whirrfftt

What's that sound?

It's a digger.

Putt - putt - verrrmmm - verrrmmm - verrrmmm

What's that sound?

It's a motorcycle.

Chugga - chugga - chugga - chooo - chooo

What's that sound?

It's a train.

Wee - owww
 - wee - owww
  - wee - owww

What's that sound?

It's a police car.

uhn - uhn - uhn

clank - clank -clank

What's that sound?

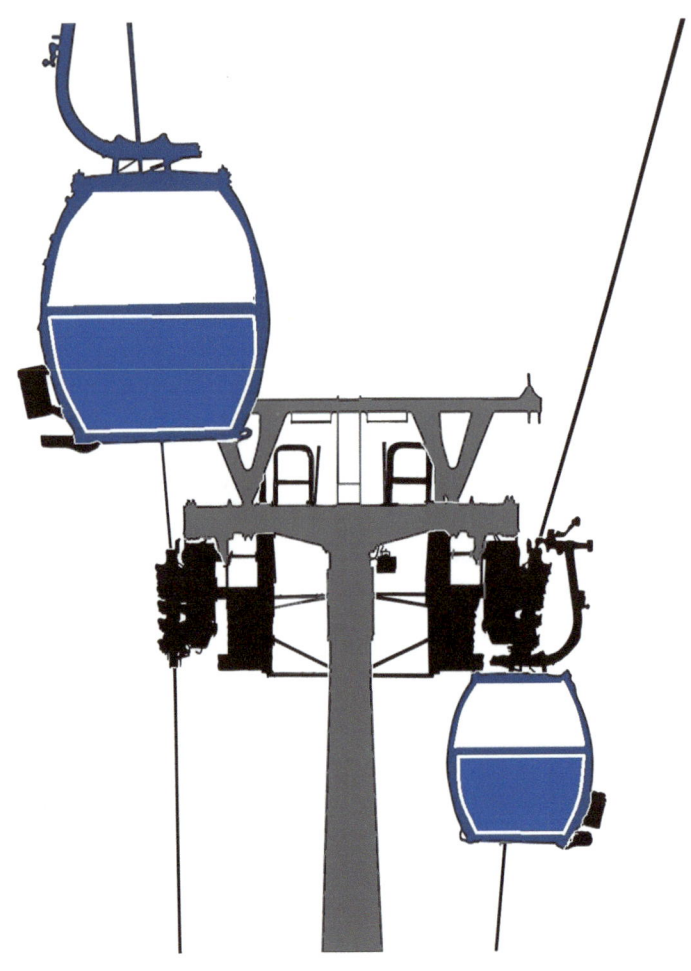

It's a gondola.

bwAAAAAAAHHHP

bwAAAAAAAAHHHP

What's that sound?

It's a ferry.

Rah - ah - ah - ah

Rah - ah - ah - ah

What's that sound?

It's a street sweeper.

shuh - huh - huh

shuh - huh - huh

What's that sound?

It's a tug boat.

Erm - mm - ursh
- clang - clang
- erm - ursh
- clang - clang

What's that sound?

It's a garbage truck.

Ding - dong - ding

zee - eee - eee.

What's that sound?

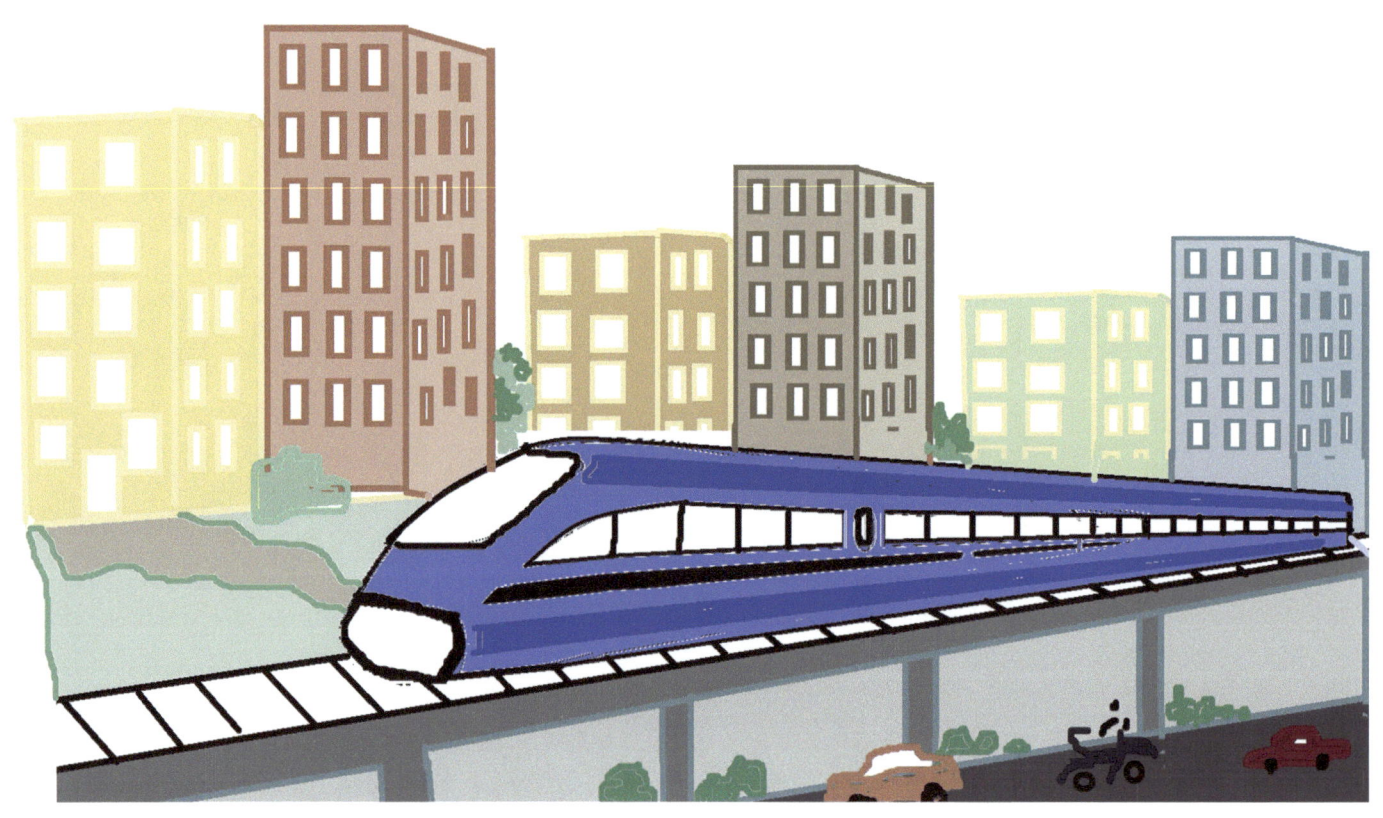

It's a skytrain.

www.ingramcontent.com/pod-product-compliance
Lightning Source LLC
Chambersburg PA
CBHW042125040426
42450CB00002B/78